The Candid Photographer

PAUL WAHL

CHILTON BOOKS

A DIVISION OF CHILTON COMPANY

Publishers

Philadelphia

New York

Library of Congress Catalog Card No. 63-16483

First Printing

Contents

1. INTRODUCTION TO CANDID PHOTOGRAPHY

A candid photograph is simply an informal picture of an unposed subject. By this broad definition, much of what is best in modern photography comes into the candid category. If the photographer is unobtrusive, his subjects, even when aware of his presence, soon become oblivious to the camera, can be caught unposed, and, hence, naturally represented. Today, the term "candid" ofttimes is applied also to what might more properly be called "pseudo-candids," pictures so cleverly posed that they look unposed. Such photographs, not uncommon in advertising, require a high degree of talent in front of, as well as behind the camera. True candid photos, however, are not in any way contrived—they are pictures of *things as they are.*

Like truth, which it should represent, the candid photograph is not always a pleasant, pretty, or amusing thing. It may derive its impact from the sad, tragic, ugly, brutal, or vulgar, for life is all of these too. Some pictures are "stoppers" with instant eye appeal to attract the attention of even the most casual viewer. Others more subtly invite contemplation of the stories they tell and often bring you back to look at them again and again. If candid photographs are revealing of the subject, they are perhaps even more revealing of the photographer. As an extension of his eye and brain, the lens "sees" as the photographer does—dispassionately, sympathetically, cruelly, with love, with hate. In his pictures, he often exposes his own personality, as much as that of his subject, to the sensitive viewer.

Commenting on the effect of the invention of photography on painting, John Canaday, art critic of *The New York Times,* has written: ". . . the photograph, which does such a magnificent job when it works candidly, has robbed the painter of his reasons for being when he works as a commentator on the current scene."* The portrayal of reality, the capture of a moment of life in progress—these things the camera does best. On the other hand, expressions of the abstract are better left to the painter and the sculptor. Although the point quite probably is endlessly debatable, I believe that it is in candid pictures that photography makes its greatest contribution to art. To those who would argue that many a good candid photograph is fortuitous, I say that it seems strange that these happy accidents happen again and again to the same people.

Despite the fact that, for more than half a century, many outstanding photographs have been made using essentially candid techniques, this

* *The New York Times,* July 1, 1962.

kind of photography—indeed, the very word *candid*—retains today something of the ill fame it acquired in its earlier days. With the growth in popularity of the 35mm camera, there began in the 1930's the modern "Candid Camera Craze," a revival of the similar "Detective Camera" fad of the 1880–1900 period. To the general public, the candid cameraman was a pest who sneaked about, maliciously poking his lens into other people's business with the intent of recording their most embarrassing moments and capturing on film every undignified or unattractive expression and attitude. It was only natural that people came to resent the actions of these photographic practical jokers as humiliating and invasions of privacy. Thus, because its techniques were exploited—perverted—by some irresponsible practitioners, candid photography unfortunately became pervaded with the bad odor which, to some extent at least, still clings to it today. When I first announced my intention to do this book, I was admonished by people in photographic circles to avoid the use of the word "candid," especially in the title. No one, however, was able to suggest an acceptable synonym for this generally understood term.

Properly employed by a photographer with understanding and sympathy for his subjects—a decent regard for human dignity—candid techniques produce important historic documents, meaningful social commentaries, and by far the most interesting pictures of people—portraits alive with personality and character. Happily, in the same era in which some cameramen were giving candid photography a bad name, others were helping it to grow up by using its methods in making some of the greatest photographs of all time. Among the outstanding photographic careers that began in the twenties and thirties were those of Margaret Bourke-White, Brassai, Henri Cartier-Bresson, Robert Doisneau, David Douglas Duncan, Alfred Eisenstaedt, Dorothea Lange, and Erich Salomon; representative examples of their work appear in these pages.

The term "candid photograph" is supposed to have been coined some thirty-odd years ago by a British editor to describe the striking, unposed portraits of world leaders made by the great pioneer photojournalist, Erich Salomon. As a matter of fact, however, candid photography greatly antedates Dr. Salomon. In 1839, Louis-Jacques-Mandé Daguerre announced his invention of the Daguerreotype Process, first practicable system of photography. That same year—quite by accident, it would appear—Daguerre took the first photograph of a human being. Since it is unlikely that the subject knew he was being photographed, this daguerreotype might be considered the first "candid camera shot." Despite this early start, it was not until 40 years later that candid photography, as we know it, became practical. By 1878, dry plates, introduced by the inventor Richard Leach Maddox in 1871, had become fast enough to permit "instantaneous exposures" of 1/25 second. Cameras could be hand held. No longer needing a tripod, the photographer was able to range freely and more or less unobtrusively with his hand camera, making snapshots of whatever subjects caught his eye.

4

Louis-Jacques-Mandé Daguerre.
PARIS BOULEVARD. 1839.

Courtesy George Eastman House

Detail, THE FIRST CANDID CAMERA SHOT.

During the 1880's, "detective" or "spy" cameras became the rage. For surreptitious photography, cameras were concealed in books, paper parcels, walking sticks, behind cravats, and even hidden in the tops of bowler hats; especially popular were cameras made in the semblance of pocket watches. Perhaps the wildest idea of that era was a camera disguised as, of all things, a revolver! Notable among detective-camera users was Paul Martin. Armed with a Fallowfield "Facile" camera disguised as a suitcase, this Londoner, able to move in the midst of his subjects without arousing suspicion, made a unique series of unposed photographs documenting the street life of the city. These pictures, and his unusual studies of streets at night, won Martin world-wide acclaim. Around the turn of the century, the detective-camera vogue had virtually faded away, but many serious photographers—among them, Arnold Genthe, Lewis W. Hine, Jacob A. Riis, Alfred Stieglitz, and Paul Strand—were employing candid techniques.

Just as the development of fast dry plates and the detective camera heralded the Victorian period in the history of candid photography, so the introduction in 1924 of the Leica, first practical 35mm camera, brought about a revolution in photographic technique and opened the modern phase of candid photography. The attributes of the 35mm camera —small size, inconspicuous appearance, fast lens and shutter, quiet operation, ease of handling, large magazine capacity, etc.—make it ideally suited to candid work, offering the photographer a unique degree of flexibility. That much of today's best camera work is candid is due largely to the widespread use of 35mm equipment.

It is the purpose of this book to provide an introduction to the art of candid photography, its techniques and matériel. Reproduced in these pages are some 50 outstanding photographs, among them a number of masterpieces of camera art; all, I think, are worthy to serve as models of candid photography. Carefully studied, these pictures will tell you more about this art than would many thousands of words.

LEICA MODEL A
1924

Courtesy E. Leitz, Inc.

6

Paul Martin. MAGAZINE SELLER. Ludgate Circus, London, c. 1895.

Courtesy The Museum of Modern Art

Alfred Stieglitz. VENETIAN BOY. 1887.

Alfred Stieglitz Collection, George Eastman House

By permission of Miss Georgia O'Keeffe

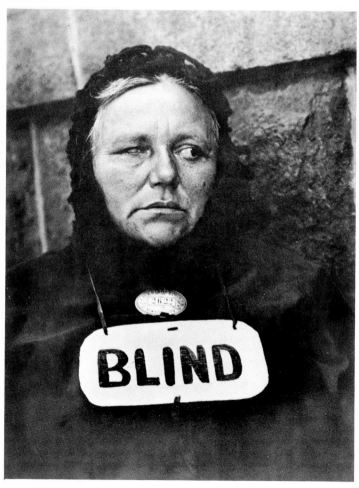

Paul Strand. BLIND. 1916.

Jacob A. Riis. RIVINGTON STREET DUMP. New York, c. 1890.

Mrs. E. A. Austen. ORGAN GRINDER AND HIS WIFE. New York, 1897.
The Library of Congress

Arnold Genthe. PIGTAIL PARADE. San Francisco, c. 1897.
Courtesy The Art Institute of Chicago

11

Eugène Atget, UMBRELLA PEDDLER. 1910.

The George Eastman House Collection

Eugène Atget. BROTHEL, VERSAILLES. c. 1920.

The George Eastman House Collection

Lewis Hine. LITTLE SPINNER IN A CAROLINA COTTON MILL. 1909.

The George Eastman House Collection

Lewis Hine. SIDEWALKS OF NEW YORK. 1910.

The George Eastman House Collection

2. CANDID TECHNIQUES

There is an inborn aptitude that makes a great photographer, but anyone willing to put forth the necessary effort can become a competent photographer. Candid photography can be learned, but I seriously doubt that it can be taught. All any teacher, or a book such as this, can do is point you in the right direction. Reading "how to" helps to a degree, but proficiency in candid photography is gained by taking pictures, by making mistakes, recognizing and correcting them.

Prerequisite to success in this or any other branch of photography is, of course, mastery of your camera. If you are to shoot fast enough to capture "the decisive moment," the manipulations involved in the operation of the camera must be second nature to you. Think how automatically you operate the controls of an automobile or, perhaps, a typewriter; you can do the same with a camera.

The first and most important step toward mastery of your camera is to become thoroughly familiar with the details and procedures of its operation. This cannot be accomplished by a cursory reading of the instruction manual or a half-hour briefing in the camera store. You have to sit down with the camera and the instruction booklet before you, and go over each detail until you are sure you understand it. No camera is too complicated for the average person to learn to operate in a short time, even if he is inexperienced with things photographic.

After you have learned how to work the different controls, practice operating them until their manipulation becomes thoroughly familiar to you. Load and unload a film until you are able to accomplish these operations with ease and speed. Expert camera handling can be quite impressive to watch, yet it is a skill fairly easy to acquire. From the beginning adopt a definite routine and stick to it; always perform the operations in the same sequence. Just as dry firing helps to perfect marksmanship with a rifle or pistol, so will dry runs with an unloaded camera aid you in developing facility in its handling. Any display of ineptness on the part of the photographer is bound to have an adverse effect on the attitude of his subject. In the case of the candid photographer, camera fumbling will attract unwanted attention.

Beyond mastery of the mechanics of camera operation, which any fairly bright 12-year-old can accomplish, the candid photographer must have a good, basic knowledge of the photographic process—how photography works, and an understanding of the capabilities and limitations of his camera and film. A basic course in photography is not within the scope of this book. If you need such a course, there are plenty of excellent manuals providing instruction in the fundamentals. You will find some included among the titles listed on the back cover of this book. Highly recommended is *How to Make Good Pictures,* published by Eastman Kodak Company and available at most photo dealers.

In my opinion, the single, most useful volume for any photographer to own is *The Focal Encyclopedia of Photography,* published in England by Focal Press Ltd. and distributed in the U.S. by The Macmillan Company.

Armed with facility in camera handling and operation, plus an understanding of the basics of photography, the neophyte candid cameraman must acquire the most important ability of all, he must learn to "see" pictures, to recognize instantly in any given situation the elements of a good photograph. To a degree, this ability can be acquired, but here is where the "inborn aptitude," mentioned in the first paragraph of this section, comes in. *Instinct,* I think, makes the difference between the journeyman candid photographer and the master—a Cartier-Bresson or an Eisenstaedt. Surely experience helps a great deal, but instinct is the extra that makes for great pictures. Obviously, we can't all be Cartier-Bressons or Eisenstaedts, but anyone can become a reasonably competent candid photographer.

How do you learn to "see" pictures? Much can be learned in the study of outstanding candid pictures and, to that end, more than half of the pages of this book are devoted to such photographs. I recommend, as profitable to the aspiring candid cameraman, the pleasant occupation of looking at photos reproduced in books and magazines. You will find many good candid shots published in periodicals such as *Life* and *Look,* as well as in the various photographic journals issued here and abroad. Especially excellent sources are the several photo annuals, e.g., *The German Photographic Annual, Photography Annual* (U.S.), *Photography Year Book* (G.B.), *U.S. Camera Annual.* The last has been issued for more than 25 years and your public library may have back numbers available.

In looking at these pictures, notice how many are photographs of rather ordinary, everyday subjects—the kind you may pass up because you fail to see their picture possibilities—found in what Stieglitz called "the exploration of the familiar." You don't have to be there when something unusual occurs, or travel to faraway places to make great candid photos. Opportunities are all around you; it's just a matter of learning to recognize them.

Your skill as a candid photographer develops through taking pictures—lots of them—as often as possible. *Make it a habit never to be without a camera.* When it is inconvenient or impossible to carry a larger camera, you always can take along a subminiature.

ERICH SALOMON
Father of Modern Candid Photography
1886-1944

During the thirties, Erich Salomon won world-wide acclaim for his unique photoreportage of international conferences and especially for his candid portraits of the famous personalities of the day. In this 1931 picture, Dr. Salomon is shown with the Ermanox camera which he used in much of his work. This camera used 4.5x6cm glass plates and had a 100mm $f/2$ lens, considered very fast in those days.

Courtesy Peter Hunter and Magnum Photos

Carrying the Camera

This may sound a bit *too* basic—like a cookbook giving instructions on how to boil water—but it really isn't. If you still carry your camera in an ever-ready case or if you load yourself down with a big gadget bag full of things you don't need, believe me, *you* should read this section carefully. An expert photographer, amateur or pro, rarely carries his camera in an ever-ready case. He has learned, probably through bitter experience, that the ever-ready case is *never* ready. By the time you get the front unbuttoned and out of the way, the picture is lost. The proper way to carry a camera is uncased, suspended from a neckstrap. Avoid neck-chains and straps with swiveled snap-fasteners; such hardware usually is not very strong (the tiny pins holding the swivels are prone to shearing off) and will rub against the camera body with disastrous effects on the finish. (I've seen cameras not only scratched but actually dented by continual contact with such fasteners.) The best type of strap is a simple one made of soft leather and fitted with split rings for attaching to the eyelets of the camera. Strap length should be such that, when suspended from the shoulder, the camera hangs with its baseplate at the level of the photographer's belt.

If you want to be inconspicuous, *like a candid photographer should,* don't wear your camera like a lavaliere—suspended from the strap around your neck and reposing on your bosom. *Leica Photography* magazine once called this the "I am a camera" method. With the protruding lens pointing indiscriminately at all and sundry, this procedure is guaranteed to spook your subjects. An ancillary disadvantage: some irate lens victim might notice that the neckstrap, thus worn, can double nicely as a garrote!

Another camera-carrying fashion to be eschewed is the "Sam Browne" method (after the military-and-police belt of the same name) which, from my observations, seems to be favored by tourists. The strap, pulled over the head, crosses the chest and back from one shoulder, with the camera resting under the opposite armpit. It should be obvious that this arrangement is both awkward and uncomfortable. If you won't take my word for it, please try the "Sam Browne" method yourself, preferably with your camera in an ever-ready case.

Some photographers prefer to have their camera in hand, at their side, always ready to raise into picture-taking position. The strap is wrapped around the wrist as a safety measure and to provide some support, à la rifle sling, while shooting. A firm grip is taken on the right end of the camera body with the right hand. Carried thusly, the camera is rather vulnerable, especially in crowds, but this method certainly is unobtrusive and many people use it, at least occasionally, when grab shots are anticipated.

The best way to carry a camera, I think, is slung by the strap from your left shoulder; your arm, in front or in back of the camera, affords some protection. Both hands are free, if needed for other tasks, and the camera can be brought into action rapidly. Provided that the lens does not protrude too far from the camera body, making the unit overly bulky,

Erich Salomon. QUAI D'ORSAY RECEPTION. August, 1931.

Aristide Briand, French Foreign Minister, spots Dr. Salomon at the reception
from which photographers were barred, points him out and is himself caught
by Salomon's camera. *Courtesy Peter Hunter and Magnum Photos*

Erich Salomon. CONFERENCE IN ROME. August, 1931.

Courtesy Peter Hunter and Magnum Photos

a good place to wear a 35mm camera is under your jacket; in this way, it is both protected and concealed, cannot slip off your shoulder or swing out and strike something if you should turn quickly. The coat must, of course, be loose-fitting and unbuttoned, if you are to get the camera out fast. When working with two cameras, I find it best to sling one from each shoulder; any other arrangement seems to lead to strap tangling and camera bumping.

Incidentally, if you sling your camera, at waist level, from your left shoulder, the strap can be used very effectively as an aid to steady holding at slow shutter speeds or with long lenses. When ready to shoot, slip your right hand inside the strap, pulling it down and holding it flat against the right end of the camera body. Bring the camera forward and up to your eye; the strap is pulled tight under the left armpit, helping to hold the camera steady.

All of the foregoing camera-carrying methods apply primarily to 35mm rangefinder and prism-reflex cameras. With the twin-lens reflex, the approved hold requires that the camera be slung from the photographer's neck and rest against his chest or abdomen. Many twin-lens reflex users seem to regard this as the only way; however, Mamiya and Rollei owners will find that special grips, offered as accessories for these cameras, provide effective means of one-hand carrying and steady holding, especially with eye-level finders.

A lens cap does not belong on a candid photographer's lens, except when it's stored away. You will not have time to remove a cap before shooting and there is always the danger, with a rangefinder camera, that you will forget to take off the cap. Naturally, you will want to protect the lens while carrying your camera uncased. I recommend the use of a screw-in UV filter on the lens; this is a "lens cap" you can shoot through. No exposure increase is required with such a filter, which can be left on at all times, regardless of the kind of film or the light. A lens shade also serves to protect the lens (or filter).

The candid cameraman should always travel light, carrying the absolute minimum of equipment. An oversized gadget bag, loaded with non-essentials, simply advertises the fact that you're on hand to take pictures. One camera, one lens (carefully selected to suit the situations anticipated), a lens shade and/or UV filter, an exposure meter, and a couple of extra films, are my basic kit for candid shooting. I think twice before adding anything else, especially if it means taking along a gadget bag.

When I do carry a gadget bag, it is one of the compact, hard-sided, leather cases made in Germany. Mine measures, exclusive of the front pocket, about 9½x6¾x4¾". Original interior fittings have been removed and the case has been partitioned to accommodate a rangefinder camera with 35mm or 50mm lens and a 105mm-equipped, single-lens reflex. Outside pocket holds exposure meter, films, and miscellaneous small accessories. When slung from the shoulder, this case opens away from the body, providing access to the contents; its snap fasteners are, I think, much preferable to the zippers common to most domestic gadget bags.

Holding the Camera

It is very important that you learn to hold your camera steadily. The chief cause of fuzzy pictures is camera shake due to unsteady holding.

Some books tell you that a tripod should be used when the exposure time is longer than about 1/30 sec. However, conditions are encountered quite frequently in available-light candid photography where slow speeds must be used. Usually, it isn't possible—or even desirable—for the candid cameraman to use a tripod; his camera is almost always hand held (occasionally, some sort of support can be extemporized). With a little practice, most people can hand hold exposures as long as 1/8 or 1/4 sec.; some experienced photographers are able to hold a camera steady for a half-second or longer.

To check your steadiness, tape a small mirror to the front of your camera and direct the beam of a flashlight into it; squeeze the shutter release as though making a picture and see if the spot of light, reflected by the mirror, moves to any great extent. Practice until you can hold the camera steady for long exposures.

The foregoing remarks about shutter speeds and the hand-held camera do not apply to the use of the longer long-focus lenses. On a 35mm camera, a 105mm lens probably will not give you any trouble, but longer lenses will require speeds of 1/30 or faster, depending upon focal length, size, and weight of the objective. Some photographers can hand hold some 400mm lenses without any artificial support, but I consider 300mm the longest focal length practical for hand-held operation. A 300mm or 400mm, generally speaking, calls for a shutter speed of at least 1/125 sec. Incidentally, a very handy gadget for steadying hand-held exposures with long lenses is the Schiansky Staticfix-203; a sort of "shoulder-pod" made of light-metal rods, it does the job of a shoulder stock, yet weighs only about 4 ounces and folds to pocket size (distributed by E. Leitz, Inc., New York).

Author's GECO "Reporter" Camera Case. Custom fitted to accommodate two 35mm cameras, RF and SLR.

21

The 35mm rangefinder camera or single-lens reflex, operated at eye level, is held firmly in both hands. Avoid too tight a grip as any tension will induce a tremor that may result in camera shake. Press the back of the camera against your eyebrow and the side of the nose. Arms are held close to the body and braced against the chest. For good balance, it is best to stand flat-footed with legs apart. When slow shutter speeds must be used, try to find something to lean on or against.

On most current 35mm cameras, the shutter-release button and wind lever are mounted on the right side of the top of the body, where these controls can be operated with a minimum of movement by the forefinger and thumb of the right hand, without taking the camera away from your eye. In addition to working the shutter-release button and wind lever, the right hand points the camera. With cameras having a focusing wheel (e.g., the Nikon S-3 and SP), this is operated by the third finger of the right hand and the left hand grips the lower left end of the camera body, supporting and steadying it. Where focusing is accomplished by turning a ring on the lens, a different left-hand grip is employed: the camera rests on the palm of the hand and the focusing ring is grasped with the forefinger and thumb of that hand. With long lenses, the left hand moves forward to grasp the barrel of the lens at the point of balance.

With 35mm cameras, the horizontal format seems most natural and, therefore, many photographers, not all of them novices, rarely shoot verticals. This is a serious mistake, since at least half of the subjects you will encounter can be composed more effectively in vertical format. The advisability of filling the frame with a negative as small as 24x36mm should be obvious—shooting vertical subjects in horizontal format wastes precious film area. The technique of taking vertical pictures should be mastered by every user of a 35mm camera. It may be a bit awkward at first, but you will find, after a little practice, that you can handle your camera in either a horizontal or a vertical position with equal ease.

It is desirable, I think, to employ a method of vertical holding in which the positions of both hands are altered as little as possible in turning the camera from horizontal to vertical. This will permit changing the camera position with the greatest ease and speed—important in fast shooting. The camera is rotated 90° to the left, bringing it into vertical position with the right hand on top. The camera body is gripped in the right hand with the right index finger on the shutter release and the right thumb at the wind lever. The left end of the camera body, now on the bottom, is cradled in the left palm, while the focusing ring is turned between the left thumb and forefinger.

In addition to the usual horizontal and vertical camera holding positions, a 35mm camera may be held upside down to gain height (an ancillary benefit is the added support provided by the camera back which, in this position, rests firmly against the user's forehead).

Dorothea Lange. MIGRANT MOTHER. California, 1936.

Farm Security Administration Collection,
The Library of Congress

The Candid Approach

> *In whatever picture-story we try to do, we are bound to arrive as intruders. It is essential, therefore, to approach the subject on tiptoe—even if the subject is still-life. A velvet hand, a hawk's eye—these we should all have.*
>
> —Henri Cartier-Bresson, *The Decisive Moment.*
> New York: Simon and Schuster, 1952.

Actually, there are two basic approaches: the *straight candid* and the *setup candid*. In the first, the photographer operates stealthily so that the subject remains unaware of the camera's presence. In the second, the approach is candid, but the situation is set up—although the subject is aware of the camera's presence, he comes to ignore it and goes about his normal activities as though no pictures were being taken.

The cameraman, who essays the straight candid approach, must present an appearance which will not attract attention. His attire should, as much as possible, conform with that of other persons of the locality; it should be ordinary, plain, even drab. His manner should be commonplace and he must not be conspicuous by voice or action. Although it is sometimes advisable to wear the camera under your coat, it need not, generally speaking, be concealed, but should be carried and handled casually. In this, more than any other branch of photography, complete mastery of the camera is essential; its operation must be second nature to you.

In straight candid photography, it is often necessary for the cameraman to move in close to his subjects, especially if he is using a wide-angle or normal lens. At the outset, many photographers are somewhat timid about doing this when taking pictures of strangers. As far as I know, there is only one cure for this phobia: go out and shoot such photos. Of course, you must exercise some judgment as to whom and where it might be risky to photograph in this manner. You will find that, for the most part, people aren't very observant and are unlikely to notice that you are taking pictures. If they do see you, few seem to mind being photographed, and those who do rarely object strenuously. Should someone ask you not to take his picture, it is only common courtesy to accede to his wish.

When working with a wide-angle lens, you can often move in so close that the subject will think you're shooting past him at something farther away—he can't believe that you could be photographing him at such short range.

It is most important in candid work that you avoid displaying a furtive or unsure attitude; this will give you away quicker than anything else. You must have confidence in your ability to handle any situation. Concentration on what you're doing, losing yourself in the little world of the viewfinder, will help you forget any timidity you may have felt about photographing strangers.

The use of a long-focus or telephoto lens may seem the easiest way of shooting candids—sometimes it is, but there are drawbacks. You can

Margaret Bourke-White, *Life.* FAMILY FLEEING PAKISTAN. 1947.

work at a comfortable distance from the subject and photograph him repeatedly if you wish, without much chance of being spotted. The chief problem presented by this technique is that lenses longer than about 300mm usually cannot be hand held and a tripod must be used. This means that you must find a suitable vantage point at which to set up your equipment and, thus, you're pretty well tied down. You can, however, get excellent pictures with a long-lensed camera set up in a good location such as a window overlooking a busy street. The camera should be located about 10' back from the window to avoid its being seen from the outside.

Halfway between the close-up techniques employed with wide-angle and normal lenses and the long view taken with telephotos is the use of a medium long-focus lens such as a 105mm or 135mm. With a medium-long, you can keep a respectable distance away from your subject and still get frame-filling images. While the average 200mm is a pretty big objective, most 105mm lenses aren't much larger or heavier than the normal lenses for the same camera. This makes them fairly inconspicuous and easy to handle candidly.

To be prepared for whatever picture opportunities are presented, the candid photographer should master both the close-up and long-range techniques. In the more controlled conditions of the setup candid approach, he will apply the appropriate methods of straight candid photography to get the desired candid feeling in his pictures.

The Grab Shot

This is the basic technique of the candid photographer. A high percentage of the best candid photos are grab shots. The photographic equivalent of the "fast draw," celebrated in TV westerns, the grab shot involves cutting to a minimum the time that elapses between the instant you spot a good picture possibility and the moment the shutter is released. There is no time in grab shooting for opening cases, removing lens caps, and fumbling with controls. The camera must be carried ready for action—uncased, conveniently slung from the shoulder or carried in hand, focused, aperture and shutter speed set, film transported and shutter cocked. All the photographer should have to do is point the camera in the right direction, frame the subject in the finder, and shoot. *The key to successful grab shooting is the presetting of the camera.*

If you're an experienced photographer, you probably can estimate exposures with a fair degree of accuracy when it isn't feasible to use an exposure meter. Fortunately, the wide latitude of medium-speed films, such as Kodak Plus-X Pan, provides a rather generous margin for error. You usually can anticipate the light conditions you will encounter and tentatively set lens aperture and shutter speed beforehand (the data leaflet packed with each film provides a helpful exposure table). When you arrive at the location where you will be shooting, take exposure-meter readings, if at all possible. It is desirable to check the light in various

Alfred Eisenstaedt, *Life.* CARNEGIE HALL. 1960.

27

parts of the area, noting the differences in brightness of illumination. Where brightness range is not great, you very likely can get away with using an intermediate exposure; otherwise, make mental notes of the variations and, while shooting, compensate for them by opening or stopping-down the lens diaphragm accordingly. Use the smallest aperture possible with a shutter speed fast enough to minimize camera and subject movement; the smaller aperture will, of course, give greater depth of field, insurance that your grab shots will be in acceptably sharp focus.

Prefocusing for outdoor shots, where use of a small aperture is practicable, can be simplified by using *hyperfocal distance** settings. Set the infinity mark on the distance scale opposite the *f*/stop on the depth-of-field scale and the lens is focused on the hyperfocal distance; depth of field extends from half the hyperfocal distance to infinity. For example: a 35mm lens has its aperture set at *f*/5.6; when the infinity mark is aligned with *f*/5.6, the objective is focused at the hyperfocal distance of 24′ and depth of field extends from 12′ to infinity. This, incidentally, serves to illustrate the usefulness of a wide-angle lens, with its greater-than-normal depth of field, in grab shooting. With such a lens, you can achieve virtual "universal" focus.

When working under relatively low light levels, as in most indoor photography, wide diaphragm openings are necessary. Under such conditions, the grab shooter sets his focus at the distance at which he expects to shoot—e.g., about 8′ for medium close-ups with a 50mm lens. The depth-of-field scale will show you how much leeway you have—usually very little if you're using a wide aperture. For indoor grab shooting, it is advisable to use high-speed films, such as Kodak Tri-X Pan, to gain the advantage of greater depth of field through the use of smaller apertures.

When a picture opportunity presents itself and you're not sure that your camera is properly set, don't stop to focus or reset the diaphragm and shutter; grab a shot first and then, if time permits, quickly check your settings, adjust if necessary, and take another picture. The first chance may be the only one you'll get. Even if the exposure is off and/or the lens is not correctly focused, you will, at least, have some kind of picture, and a good lab man can work wonders with a poor negative.

Form the good camera-handling habit of always advancing the film and cocking the shutter (a combined operation with most cameras) immediately after making an exposure. There is nothing more disconcerting than to line up a good shot in the viewfinder, press the shutter-release button, and have nothing happen.

---

* When a lens is focused at infinity, the distance from the camera to the near limit of the sharp field is called the *hyperfocal distance.*

Robert Doisneau. SIDE GLANCE.

Rapho Guillumette Pictures

Shooting from the Hip

This is a variation of the *grab shot,* but it is so different in concept from normal camera-handling practices that it warrants separate treatment here. Shooting from the hip, a gunfighter does not use the sights of his revolver, he just points the weapon instinctively and fires from waist level. The hip-shooting cameraman, in like manner, does not use the viewfinder.

There are times when the movement of the camera to eye level, no matter how deftly done, is a giveaway and attracts unwanted attention. Under certain circumstances, this can prove embarrassing, even dangerous. Every candid photographer should master the technique of shooting from the hip.

For hip-shooting, the use of a wide-angle lens is recommended, because its greater angular coverage and depth of field provide more liberal margins for error. The two most practical short focal lengths for the 35mm camera are 35mm and 28mm; respectively, these objectives cover approximately $2\times$ and $3\times$ the field of the standard 50mm lens. Even greater coverage is afforded by such extreme wide angles as 21mm and 25mm, but these lenses must be used more carefully than is ordinarily possible in hip-shooting if grotesquely distorted images are to be avoided.

To illustrate the coverage provided by a 35mm lens: with the camera held horizontally at waist level, an objective of this focal length will cover vertically the full standing figure of a man 5' 9" tall at a distance of 10'. In view of the facts that, normally, such a "target" is only about 20" wide and the horizontal coverage of the lens is approximately 1½× as great as the vertical, it can be seen that any aiming problem will not be lateral.

The key to successful hip-shooting is knowing how much coverage your lens will give at various distances. This can be determined by simple experimentation. Mount your camera on a tripod and adjust the height so that the lens is at the same level as when the camera is slung from your shoulder by its carrying strap. While you look through the viewfinder, have an assistant—an average-sized adult, whose height is known to you—stand facing the camera. Direct your model to move backward or forward until his full figure, in focus, is within the frame. Read the range from the distance scale of the camera and record it for future reference. This is your basic data: how far away you must be to cover a man's full-length, standing figure. Subsequent tests should be made to determine necessary distances for seated figures, half figures, head and shoulders, etc.

With practice, you will learn to tell, at a glance, how much of the subject will be covered by your camera's field of view. You also will be able to judge whether the camera is to be held level, tilted up, or tilted down to get the desired picture. The ability to judge distance accurately is important. Practice estimating distances in the range in which you will be working (you can use the rangefinder and distance scale of your camera to check your accuracy).

Needless to say, when hip shots are contemplated, the camera must be ready for action. Any of the methods suggested in the section *Carrying*

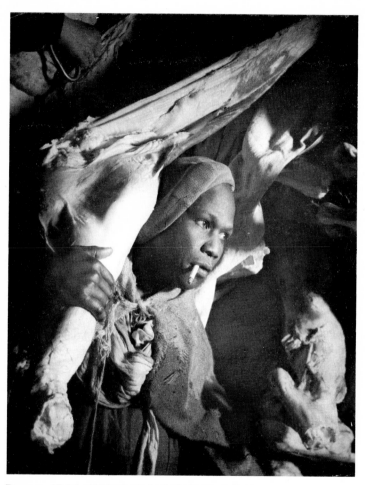

Brassai. ARAB PORTER IN LES HALLES, PARIS.

Rapho Guillumette Pictures

the Camera, may be employed. If you wear the camera slung from your shoulder, under your jacket, you can pull it out, steady it against your body, snap the picture, and return the camera to its hiding place under the coat. Some cameras, of course, are too bulky to be concealed in this manner. A favorite method with many pros is to carry the camera at the side, in hand, with strap wrapped around the wrist; from this position, it can be moved quickly and unobtrusively to waist level for a fast grab shot. With the camera slung from the shoulder, outside the jacket, you can either pull the camera around in front of your body to make a shot or leave it at your hip. From the latter position, it can be directed at your subject while you face away, looking innocently at something else. If you're close to the subject, sometimes the self-timer can be employed for a "no-hands" shutter release. With the camera away from the subject, cock the self-timer; let your arm hang at your side with the side of the lens mount resting against it (the sunshade will keep your sleeve from getting in the way) for support; press the self-timer release button, then slowly (you don't want the camera swinging) turn around so that the lens is pointing at the subject while you face away at a 90° angle.

In the beginning, you will find it helpful in perfecting your camera handling to practice in front of a mirror. This will enable you to check both your aim and whether or not the camera is held straight. It is essential that you learn to direct the camera by feel alone; looking down at it might prove a giveaway. Another practice aid is a small flashlight attached to the camera and adjusted so that its beam corresponds as closely as possible with the lens axis. The spot of light provides indication of the accuracy of your camera pointing. Useful in dry runs as well as in actual tests on film is a paper "man" target of the type used by police for combat pistol-shooting courses; these targets are obtainable from gun shops and dealers in police equipment and supplies. The target, a life-size silhouette, can be hung at levels to simulate standing or seated subjects. It can also be used for tests to determine the covering power of your lens.

Although the technique of photography-without-using-the-viewfinder has been referred to as "shooting from the *hip,*" it is obvious from the foregoing that most often the camera will be positioned at the photographer's midriff. However, as you become more confident of your proficiency in "aiming blind," you will find other applications for these basic methods. For example, the camera may be held overhead at arms' length to shoot over the heads of a crowd or over a wall. Pictures can be made with the camera standing innocently alone on a table, a chair, even on the floor or ground; "no hands" operation is made possible through the use of the self-timer. Before putting your camera aside casually—and carefully pointed at the subject—cock the self-timer; as you put the camera down, release the self-timer. Few people are observant enough to notice its sound or the movement of the lever.

Frankly, shooting from the hip is somewhat hit-or-miss. The number of hits depends upon your skill—and luck! No matter how expert you are, there will be misses. In press photographers' parlance, such blind grab

Henri Cartier-Bresson. LOURDES.

Magnum Photos

shots are called "Hail Marys"—you say a prayer when you take the picture. The ability to shoot from the hip with a fair degree of accuracy certainly is an asset to the candid photographer, but such techniques are to be reserved for those occasions when surer methods cannot be used.

The Right-Angle Shot

In making the right-angle shot, the camera is turned so that the lens is pointed to the side, in the direction of the unsuspecting subject, while the photographer faces straight ahead, but watches a right-angle view of the subject in the viewfinder. This technique, generally speaking, is best suited to the twin-lens reflex which, of all conventional cameras, is the least awkward to handle for such shooting. You can, of course, use a single-lens reflex having either a waist-level finder or a right-angle viewing attachment for the pentaprism finder; an accessory angle viewfinder permits the use of a rangefinder camera in making right-angle shots. Some models of the Robot camera have built-in provision for right-angle viewing.

For many years, users of waist-level reflexes have employed the "fake lens" technique in right-angle shooting. The phony optic, usually nothing more than an appropriately sized lens shade (sometimes combined with a filter for a properly "glassy" look), is fastened on the side of the camera. With a Rollei or similar twin-lens reflex, this is a very simple matter—the shade is slipped on the focusing knob.

In use of this arrangement, the photographer faces in the direction of the fake lens, presumably making a picture of another subject, while the real lens, at the side, is pointing at the actual subject. This method often

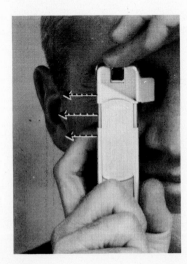

MINOX RIGHT-ANGLE
FINDER MIRROR

works quite well and sometimes permits the photographer to move in closer than would be possible without the fake lens to heighten the illusion that the camera is pointed elsewhere than at its true subject.

Whether or not you use a fake lens, the success of the right-angle shot depends a good deal on how familiar the subjects are with cameras. A person having even a slight acquaintance with photography is quite likely to notice that your camera is turned sideways and its lens is facing him, unless you keep your distance.

The camera I prefer for such shooting is the Minox with its right-angle finder mirror attached. This unit is especially effective—because of its very small size and unconventional appearance, it can be used undetected as close as an arm's length away from the subject.

Ray G. Jones,
Salt Lake City
Deseret News.
ILLEGAL GAMBLING.
Minox Photo.

Courtesy Minox Corp.

The Hidden Camera

Under certain circumstances, it may be advisable, even imperative for the photographer's safety, that the camera be concealed. Ingenious under-cover photographers have hidden cameras behind a variety of disguises, usually devising camouflage appropriate to the particular situation.

The famed Erich Salomon took a "no pictures" rule as a challenge to his ingenuity—which was considerable. He had an uncanny knack for gaining admittance and was a master of hidden-camera techniques. Dr. Salomon photographed the U.S. Supreme Court in session, using a camera hidden in a sling supporting his "injured" arm.* Three mathematics books, glued together in a stack and hollowed out to conceal a camera, provided the device by which he was able to make pictures of gambling in the Casino at Monte Carlo. At a banquet attended by President Herbert Hoover, who seems to have taken a very dim view of candid photography,

---

* Using a Leica rigged inside her handbag, this same feat was accomplished by the wife of photojournalist Thomas D. McAvoy, one of the four original *Life* photographers.

Salomon hid his camera in a vase of flowers, a few feet away from the President's place at the table, and snapped the shutter with a long cable release. Erich Salomon's exploits in this area of photography have become legendary and it is now difficult to distinguish between the apocryphal and the true; however, it can be said that, judging from the latter, most of the former actually might have happened!

On Friday, the 13th of January, 1928, the New York *Daily News* shocked its readers by front-page publication of one of the more controversial, and grisly, hidden-camera pictures of all time, Tom Howard's photograph of the electrocution of Ruth Snyder at Sing Sing on the night of the 12th.* It was the first picture made of an execution at that prison and the first of a woman's electrocution. Because of the State's ban on photography in the death house, Howard's camera had to be hidden where it would pass unnoticed during routine frisking by prison officials. A miniature camera with a single glass plate (probably an Ermanox, judging from descriptions) was strapped to the photographer's left leg, just above the ankle, with a cable release extending up the leg and into the pants pocket. He was to raise his trouser leg to uncover the lens, aim the camera at the subject by pointing his foot, and make the exposure (about 5 seconds). The considerable planning by the *News'* staff and Howard's hours of practice with his hidden camera paid off. When the executioner threw the switch, sending the lethal current surging through Ruth Snyder's body, Tom Howard shot his picture, capturing a truly "decisive moment"—the instant of death.

Hidden-camera techniques are not limited to still photography. Not long ago, CBS-TV produced a documentary, "Biography of a Bookie Joint," including on-the-spot, candid motion pictures with sound. Jay McMullen, producer of the show, entered the bookie joint with a Fairchild Cinephonic 8mm sound camera concealed in a lunch pail and controlled by a remote switch in his pocket. In the dimly lighted, smoke-filled store back room, McMullen recorded the sights and sounds of illicit gambling operations.

Whether the means of concealment is simple or elaborate, the cover employed should be some familiar, everyday item that will not attract attention or arouse suspicion: a paper sack, a paper-wrapped parcel, a lunch box, a brief or attaché case, a handbag, a portable radio, a flashlight, or a cigarette package. Frequently used is a sling, or even a plaster cast, for a "broken" arm. In most instances, it will be necessary to construct a frame—a simple affair of wood ordinarily suffices—to hold the camera in a fixed position. Where access to the release button is not convenient and use of a cable release is not feasible, an extension push-rod or some other arrangement must be provided. A hole to permit the lens to "look out" is needed; this should be as inconspicuously located as possible, perhaps where it can be covered by the hand or held toward the body.

* After a sensational trial, Mrs. Snyder and Judd Gray were convicted of the murder of her husband and sentenced to death in the electric chair at the Ossining, N.Y., penitentiary.

Ken Heyman. SALUTE.

Rapho Guillumette Pictures

With certain kinds of cover—for example, a paper sack or paper-wrapped parcel—the lens hole should look like an accidentally acquired puncture or tear.

The spotlight of an automobile has been used by criminal investigators as a hiding place for a camera equipped with a wide-angle lens. Inside-controlled, the spotlight head turns 360°, permitting the camera to traverse a wide area. Such an installation requires the services of a good mechanic. The effectiveness of such units has been proved in surveillance work by law enforcement officers and, under certain conditions, might be useful to the candid photographer.

Small cameras, especially subminiatures, are well adapted to concealment. When cameras with conventional shutter-cocking/film-transport systems are hidden, it usually is difficult to get at these controls and, thus, the photographer may be limited to one shot. Where several pictures must be made in sequence, a motor-driven camera is indicated. The chief drawback of motor-driven cameras in undercover photography is the operating noise which, in close quarters, might be noticed by subjects.

With a 35mm or subminiature camera, even when it is necessary to work unobserved, elaborately contrived camouflage is rarely required. Extensive use in undercover work has established that an inconspicuous camera of these types need not masquerade as something else. Many pros favor all-black cameras as being less noticeable than those with the conventional chrome-finished metal parts. Black cameras are most effective when the users wear dark clothing and dark gloves. Except for some of the bulkier models, a 35mm can be worn, slung from the shoulder, under your coat, quickly pulled out for a grab shot and returned to its hiding place. Subminiatures, such as the Minox, are easily pocketed or hidden in the hand.

A ruse, proved effective with the Minox, is to pretend that it is a cigarette lighter that doesn't work. Hold it up to an unlit cigarette, lens pointed at the subject, and press the shutter release. When it doesn't light, you frown and fiddle with your Minox "lighter" as a cover for performing the push-pull required to advance the film and cock the shutter for the next shot. These actions are so natural and familiar that you can usually get away with taking several pictures in this manner—until some helpful soul comes over with a light. The Minox, incidentally, saw espionage service with both sides during World War II. Japanese intelligence agents added realism to the lighter trick by using an 8mm subminiature camera built into a working cigarette lighter that looked like a slightly oversized copy of the Zippo; a similar camera-lighter, the Echo-8, is now on the U.S. market.

With a hidden camera, you employ the same basic techniques as in shooting from the hip, since usually you will not be able to use the viewfinder. *A word of warning:* until you become experienced at this sort of thing, your handling of the disguised camera may be awkward due to self-consciousness; this can defeat the very purpose of the concealment by attracting attention and, quite possibly, giving away the ruse.

David Moore. LOURDES.

Available Light

Although so well entrenched in the language of photography that it must be used, this term really is a misnomer. Taken literally, "available light" could be whatever means of illumination is at hand: a vast battery of studio flood- and spotlights, electronic flash units, or even the sun might be referred to as "available." However, in the sense in which it is commonly used in photographic parlance, available light means the existing illumination of a given situation. The available-light photographer avoids the use of flash, flood, etc., to augment existing light; he works under the conditions in which he finds his subject. Available-light techniques permit more natural pictures, especially since the subject is not disturbed by the intrusion of bright floods or flash into his normal environment. The successful candid photographer usually is, perforce, an available-light photographer.

Fast lenses, fast films, and special developing techniques (to be used only when absolutely necessary), make it possible to produce usable photographs under the most difficult existing-light conditions. It is, generally speaking, quite true that *if you can see it, you can photograph it.*

Coupled with an ultra-high-speed film such as Agfa Isopan Record (ASA EI 650*), an $f/3.5$ objective is fast enough for nearly all available-light situations. With Isopan Record, a match, held six inches from the subject, furnishes sufficient light to make a portrait with an exposure of 1/50 sec at $f/4$. However, if you plan to do much work of this type, you may prefer a faster lens in the $f/1.4$–$f/2$ class. These larger apertures permit shorter exposures, making it easier to hand hold, and sometimes allow the use of a slower film for better picture quality. For available-light color photography, a fast lens is pretty much of a must.

When working under moderately low levels of light, it is suggested that a medium-speed film (e.g., Kodak Plus-X Pan) be used, with normal development. Reserve faster films and speed-gaining development for the more difficult conditions where some sacrifice of quality can be tolerated.

Candid Portraits

> *O wad some Pow'r the giftie gie us*
> *To see oursels as others see us!*
> —Robert Burns, *To a Louse*

We have had this gift—*Photography*—for nearly 125 years now, but, unlike the poet Burns, most people don't want to see themselves as others see them. Each of us has a mental self-portrait—usually a flattering one—that is an idealized version of the image he sees in his mirror. To begin with, the face you know as yours is not the one others see, since the mirror image is laterally reversed. Only in a straight photograph do you see your

* Suggested re-rating: normal-contrast subjects, EI 1600 to 2000; low-contrast subjects, EI 3200 to 4000.

David Douglas Duncan, *Life.* CHRISTMAS IN KOREA, 1950.

"This is the face of a man who eats frozen rations in the snow and who may be interrupted at any moment to run, to fight or to die."

—*Life*, December 25, 1950.

real likeness. Long ago, portraitists recognized these facts and found that, quite often, a photograph rejected by the sitter could be converted into a satisfactory portrait by simply printing the negative from the wrong side. The candid photographer usually strives to achieve an honest portrayal of his subject and, more often than not, gets no thanks for his pains.

While I certainly do not advocate that the candid portraitist resort to the tricks of the studio to flatter his subjects inordinately, he can show, without compromising his honesty as a photographer, a little kindness and respect for human dignity by trying to portray people at their best and not at their worst.

The most interesting pictures of people are those which succeed in capturing the personality and character of the subject. Rarely accomplished in formal portraiture, this quality is more frequently seen in candid portraits.

While it is often desirable that those being photographed are unaware of the camera's presence, this is by no means essential to obtaining natural portraits. Use of a small camera has the effect of minimizing camera shyness and, although aware of the camera's presence, the subject soon becomes oblivious to it—provided that the cameraman does not obtrude. Working with a 35mm camera, preferably under existing illumination in the subject's home or other familiar surroundings, you can obtain exceptional results. Take advantage of your camera's large magazine capacity to shoot your subject in a variety of poses and from different angles. You will find that even camera-shy subjects, who tend to freeze before the shutter is released, will relax after a number of exposures are made.

An attractive assistant, who is an engaging talker or a good listener, can be a big help in drawing the subject's attention away from the camera. It is even better if the subject can be persuaded to forget about your presence and go about his normal activities while you shoot.

I prefer 35mm cameras for candid portraiture and find that the 35mm and 105mm focal lengths are ideal for my work. The 35mm lens is used for full-length shots and in situations where it is desirable to include background details to relate the subject to his environment. For head shots, the 105mm does the job perfectly; the relatively shallow depth of field gives an attractive plasticity to portraits produced with this medium-long-focus lens.

Truly candid portraits are often made from a distance. Photojournalists now use 180mm to 400mm long-focus lenses, even super-telephotos up to 1000mm, for making revealing close-up candid portraits at long range.

Brian Brake. NIGERIAN GIRL.

Face in the crowd shot with a 125mm lens.

Magnum Photos

Michael Rougier, *Life.*
ON A MAN'S MISSION. Hungary, November, 1956.

"Pal Pruck, 15, was one of the many brave teen-agers who fought in the rebellion. He is standing in a rubble-strewn Budapest street."

—*Life,* November 12, 1956.

Copyright 1956 Time Inc.

3. THE CANDID CAMERA

According to my dictionary, a *candid camera* is "any small camera with a fast lens, used to take informal pictures of unposed subjects." This is a good definition insofar as it accurately describes the type of camera generally considered best suited to candid photography, but there really is no such thing as a "candid camera"—the photographer, not the camera, is "candid." Outstanding candid photographs have been made with almost every kind of camera. Although most of the pictures in this book are products of either 35mm or 2¼x2¼ cameras, there are some noteworthy exceptions. *Blind* by Paul Strand was made with a 3¼x4¼ Graflex. Dorothea Lange also used a Graflex in photographing the *Migrant Mother*. Bill Gallagher's Pulitzer Prize winning shot of Adlai Stevenson with a hole in his shoe was taken with a 4x5 Speed Graphic. All of these cameras were large; none was equipped with a lens that would be considered fast by today's standards. These pictures are great because the photographers are great; their tools, while adequate, were incidental.

In candid photography, the camera to use is the one with which you are most familiar, the one whose operation has become second nature to you—provided, of course, that this camera is sufficiently versatile to handle the candid picture taking situations you expect to encounter. Before making any change in equipment, ask yourself, "Will it really help me to take better pictures?" and insist upon getting an honest answer! The following pages are devoted to discussions of equipment, especially cameras, for candid photography. In 30 years of photography (I started young!), I've taken a lot of pictures with a lot of different cameras and have formed a number of opinions that you may find interesting and possibly helpful.

Back in the 1930's when the term *candid camera* was coined, it meant the Leica or almost anything that resembled it, however slightly. Today, most candid cameramen still choose a 35mm camera with a focal-plane shutter, either the coupled-rangefinder or the single-lens reflex type. Runner-up in popularity is the 2¼x2¼ twin-lens reflex. The prospective purchaser of a 35mm SLR has a much wider choice than one who has decided upon either a 35mm RF or a 2¼x2¼ TLR. There are more than two dozen 35mm single-lens reflex cameras worthy of consideration, ranging in price from under $150 to over $500, while in 35mm RF's and 2¼x2¼ TLR's you are limited to a comparatively few makes and models.

35mm—Rangefinder or Reflex?

Regardless of which type of camera you choose, it should have a focal-plane shutter. Lens interchangeability, with a fairly wide choice of focal lengths, usually is considered essential in a 35mm camera for candid photography. This requirement virtually eliminates from consideration cameras with leaf-type shutters. While the behind-lens leaf shutter permits changing lenses (not feasible with the between-lens type), the range of focal lengths available is severely limited. The owner of any of the leading 35mm cameras with focal-plane shutters has a wide choice of objectives from extreme wide angle to super-telephoto.

Until quite recently, the coupled-rangefinder type (e.g., the Leica) was the favorite 35mm focal-plane-shutter camera with both professional and advanced amateur photographers—a position it had held for over 30 years. Today, the single-lens reflex is most popular. This change was brought about by the introduction, during the past five years, of SLR cameras of advanced design, incorporating improvements—eye-level focusing and viewing via pentaprism, automatic diaphragm lens, instant-return mirror—which effectively eliminated the major objections to the SLR system. The rangefinder camera, however, does have a number of strong points in its favor, especially for candid use.

It is acknowledged generally that with the shorter focal-length lenses, wide-angle and normal, coupled-rangefinder focusing is more accurate, as well as faster, than reflex focusing. This rangefinder accuracy, it should be noted, falls off as focal length increases and may be barely adequate for a 135mm lens at full aperture. Under adverse light conditions, it is easier to focus and view with an RF camera.

With a normal lens of large aperture (e.g., $f/1.4$) or a long-focus objective, reflex ground-glass focusing is easy because depth of field is shallow and the image moves in and out of focus quickly. When a wide-angle lens is used, the depth of field being considerable, it is difficult to find the point of sharp focus on the ground glass. The split-image range-finder, with which most SLR's are now equipped, is a help with this problem and also may speed up focusing with normal lenses. Photographers coming to the single-lens reflex from rangefinder cameras welcome the split-image rangefinder, while those experienced in ground-glass focusing with twin-lens reflex or view cameras generally prefer the full-area focusing permitted by a plain ground-glass screen. Disadvantages of the split-image rangefinder are that a well-defined straight line is required in the subject for accurate focusing, and that, at small apertures, with long lenses, or in poor light, one-half of the rangefinder image blacks out, rendering it useless. Several cameras are now equipped with central focusing grid (microprism), a device which breaks up the image into ripples when the lens is out of focus. Some SLR-users prefer this system to the conventional split-image rangefinder; others find it difficult to focus accurately with the microprism. A personal trial is indicated.

If a coupled-rangefinder camera is to be used with lenses of longer focal length than 135mm, it must be converted to a "single-lens reflex"

P. C. Lee, *Hong Kong Tiger Standard.*
REFUGEE. Hong Kong, May, 1962.

In a detention camp, Lee Ying, 19, a refugee just arrived from Red China, sobs her despair into a ragged handkerchief on learning that she is to be repatriated.

Wide World Photo

by the addition of a reflex housing. Although these reflex units have improved considerably over the years, such an arrangement is inferior to the modern 35mm SLR camera, and you can buy a good SLR body for the price of a reflex housing. Viewfinders of RF cameras are provided with bright frames delineating the fields of view of rangefinder-coupled lenses. The viewing image is 1:1, i.e., life size; however, while such viewfinders work fine for the wide-angle and normal lenses, the frames for 85mm to 135mm are quite small and composition is difficult. A zoom-type varifocal accessory finder maintains the same field frame for each focal length and varies the size and area of the image to conform to lens coverage. This certainly is a help but I find it a nuisance to have to shift my eye from the rangefinder eyepiece to a separate finder mounted above on the accessory clip.

Many candid photographers, particularly those who prefer to shoot at close range, make the 35mm focal length their normal lens instead of the traditional 50mm. Aside from the already mentioned superiority of coupled-rangefinder focusing with short focal-length lenses, there are other considerations for those who will make much use of the 35mm objective. While excellent 35mm lenses as fast as $f/1.4$ are available for the leading RF cameras, those made for SLR's usually have a relatively modest maximum aperture of $f/2.8$. This really is fast enough for most purposes, but the available-light specialist will feel the need for a 35mm lens in the $f/2$, or faster, class as much for reflex focusing and viewing under poor light conditions as for actual picture taking. The typical 35mm objective for an SLR is retrofocus (i.e., an inverted telephoto) with an automatic diaphragm; such a lens is necessarily bulky—roughly twice as large as the average 35mm for an RF camera.

Three disadvantages of the SLR, according to rangefinder-camera partisans, are size, weight, and noise. It must be admitted that single-lens reflexes usually are larger and heavier than cameras of the RF variety, but not significantly so. Take, for example, the following comparison of the Nikon S-3 (coupled-rangefinder) and F (single-lens reflex) models, cameras typical of their respective systems in size and weight. The body designs of the Nikon S-3 and F are quite similar. Approximate over-all dimensions and weights: S-3 with 50mm $f/1.4$ lens—5⅜x3³⁄₁₆x2¾″, 26 oz.; F with 50mm $f/1.4$ lens—5¾x3¹³⁄₁₆x4″, 37 oz. As to the noise factor: in single-lens reflex cameras, the operating sound level is somewhat higher than that of an RF with focal-plane shutter due to the added sounds of the mirror flipping up and down. While no SLR, as far as I know, is as quiet in operation as the most quiet rangefinder camera, none of the better reflexes are really much noisier. I have used most of the popular SLR's of the focal-plane-shutter type and do not feel that any is too large, too heavy, or too noisy for successful candid photography.

It is sometimes maintained that the rapid-return mirror (now common to nearly all SLR's), moving up before the exposure, causes the camera to vibrate, resulting in loss of sharpness in the negative image. Because of the cushioning materials and/or slowing mechanisms found in most

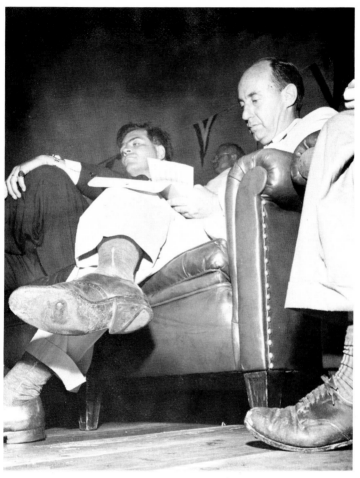

William Gallagher, *The Flint Journal,* Flint, Michigan.
ADLAI STEVENSON. 1952 Presidential Campaign. Pulitzer Prize Photo.

modern SLR's, there is very little likelihood of trouble from mirror shake.

In choosing between rangefinder and single-lens reflex 35mm cameras, the decision, I think, depends largely upon the lenses you plan to use. Either type will prove satisfactory with the normal lens—my own preference is for the SLR because I feel that ground-glass focusing is conducive to better, more imaginative composition. If the lens you use most often is a wide angle, then, for reasons already stated, you should select a coupled-rangefinder camera. On the other hand, if you use a wide-angle lens seldom or not at all, but frequently employ long-focus lenses, especially those longer than 135mm, your best bet is a single-lens reflex. If you plan to use both wide-angle and long-focus lenses extensively, the ideal—albeit expensive—solution is to have a rangefinder camera for the former and a single-lens reflex for the latter. The best alternative to the two-camera setup would be an SLR with split-image rangefinder, which many photographers find satisfactory for focusing wide-angle lenses.

To many people, price is an important consideration in the choice of a camera. Here the 35mm SLR scores heavily. Among 35mm's with focal-plane shutters, the best buys are to be found in the single-lens reflex type. You can buy a good prism reflex for under $150, about $100 less than the price of a first-class rangefinder camera.

For candid photography, it is essential that a 35mm SLR incorporate *all* of the following features: focal-plane shutter, rapid-return mirror, penta-prism finder, lens interchangeability, and automatic (or, at least, semi-automatic) diaphragm control. Don't even consider a camera—however attractively priced—that lacks any one of these features.

Which Camera Is Best?

By recent count, there are over 40 models of 35mm focal-plane shutter cameras on the market today; better than 85% of this number are single-lens reflexes. Thus, the prospective buyer of such a camera has a rather bewildering array from which to choose. It is understandable, therefore, that the question most often asked me—and, I'm sure, other photographic writers too—is *which camera is best?* By getting expert opinions, people hope to narrow the field down to workable size.

As an aid in choosing the camera best suited to your personal requirements, make a check list of the features you want and compare it with the specifications of the cameras you have under consideration. Supplementing the descriptive literature you can obtain from the manufacturers and importers, excellent sources of information are the camera reviews published in magazines such as *Modern Photography* and *Popular Photography;* both of these publications have an annual index and complete files should be available at your public library.

During the past 10 years or so, I have had an opportunity to use every one of the better 35mm cameras, rangefinder as well as reflex. Taking all factors into careful consideration, I have come to the conclusion that the Nikon F is not only the best 35mm single-lens reflex, but it is also the best

NIKON F REFLEX

To the candid photographer, nothing about a camera is more important than its handling qualities; for the required "second-nature" operation, all controls must be conveniently located. The popularity of the Nikon F is due in no small part to the fact that the designers gave it a body similar to that of the well-proved Nikon SP rangefinder model, one of the best handling 35mm cameras ever made.

The Nikon F has every feature you would expect in a top-flight SLR: pentaprism viewfinder (in this case, interchangeable with a waist-level unit and the unique Photomic combination eye-level prism finder and coupled CdS exposure meter), interchangeable focusing screens, instant-return mirror, fully automatic diaphragm control, depth-of-field preview control, 1-to-1/1000 sec. focal-plane shutter with flash sync and self-timer, rapid-wind lever, rewind crank, automatically resetting exposure counter, detachable back interchangeable with electric motor drive, plus a range of interchangeable lenses from 8mm to 1000mm focal length, as well as many useful accessories, making this a complete system of 35mm photography.

A rare combination of good design, fine workmanship, versatility, and complete reliability makes the Nikon F, in the author's opinion, the best 35mm SLR camera available today. It is ideal for candid work.

Walter E. Lautenbacher. MADAM, OUR CHILDREN LOOK AT YOU. WE BEG YOU DO NOT OFFEND THEIR INNOCENCE WITH AN INDECOROUS WAY OF DRESSING.

35mm camera for general use. This camera really has everything. Brilliantly engineered to include every important and desirable feature, its performance, optical and mechanical, is truly outstanding. A full range of excellent Nikkor lenses from 21mm to 1000mm and many useful accessories make the Nikon the most advanced and complete system of 35mm single-lens reflex photography. It is said that more pros use the Nikon F than any other 35mm reflex; popularity with men who make their living with a camera is probably the highest possible endorsement. With the better of its two fine normal lenses, the Auto-Nikkor 50mm $f/1.4$, the Nikon F costs $375.

Although I regard the Nikon F as the best 35mm SLR money can buy (incidentally, it's not the highest priced camera of its kind), I realize that not everyone can afford—or, perhaps, would care to pay—its price. To those shopping for an eye-level reflex in the $150 bracket, I recommend the Honeywell Pentax H-1 as the *best buy*. Designed with the idea of providing a compact, lightweight prism-reflex with all of the really essential features, this is a well-made, reliable camera at a modest price.

HONEYWELL
PENTAX

Three models, H-1, H-3, and H3V, share the basic Pentax design. H-1 has semi-automatic lens, 1/500-sec. shutter. H-3 has fully automatic lens, 1/1000-sec. shutter. H3V has all H-3 features plus self-timer and automatically resetting exposure counter.

You will find that the majority of professional and advanced amateur users of 35mm RF cameras work with either a Leica or a Nikon. The four current models, Leica M2S, Leica M3, Nikon S-3, and Nikon SP, range in price from under $300 to over $500. As far as results are concerned, there is ample evidence that the four are on a par. The Summicron 50mm $f/2$ lens for the Leica and the Nikkor 50mm $f/1.4$ for the Nikon are two of the finest normal lenses ever made for 35mm cameras. Both Leica and Nikon offer a complete system of photography with a wide range of lenses and accessories. To make your choice, study all four models carefully and decide which is best adapted to your personal requirements. You really can't go wrong with any one of these fine cameras.

LEICA M3

NIKON SP

Lenses for 35mm Cameras

According to the accepted rule, the *normal* or standard focal length for a given film size should be approximately equal to the diagonal of the negative. The 35mm frame measures 24x36mm and has a diagonal of 43mm. Ever since the first Leica, the traditional standard lens of 35mm cameras has been 50mm in focal length; its 45° angle of view is supposed to approximate that of the human eye and the 50mm lens is said to produce the most natural perspective. Actually, by application of the "diagonal-of-negative" rule, the 35mm focal length is almost as close to normal as is the 50mm and, indeed, nearer to it than are the 55mm and the 58mm, standard focal lengths among SLR lenses. Nevertheless, if you are going to have only one lens, it should be in the 50mm to 58mm range, as these focal lengths have been found to be better suited to general use and can handle well the majority of photographic situations.

Whether or not the 35mm is your idea of a normal lens, it certainly is virtually indispensable for close-in candid photography, especially the grab shot. The deep zone of sharp focus, characteristic of the 35mm

Merton J. Gordon

Courtesy Popular Photography Magazine

lens, eliminates the need of focusing for each shot, making your camera handling not only faster but also less conspicuous. When working by available light, a 35mm permits the use of larger apertures without too much loss in depth of field. The wider angle of view (64° compared with 45° for the 50mm) provides a greater margin for error when fast shooting prevents careful framing.

Just about as useful to the candid photographer as the 35mm wide angle are the medium long-focus lenses—85, 90, 100, and 105mm focal lengths. With a medium-long, you can keep your distance while shooting candids unnoticed, and you can take close-up portraits without risk of distortion. My own preference in this class of lens is the 105mm, which I have found to be the ideal intermediate long-focus lens. Its 2× magnification (compared with 50mm) and 23° angle of view seem to lead automatically to the frame-filling, tight composition I like to get in pictures of people. The usual medium-long lens can be hand held as easily as a normal lens. For best results, this type of objective should be used with a single-lens reflex. In RF cameras, the viewfinder image is too small for really effective use of such a lens.

The basic kit for the 35mm photographer usually consists of a wide-angle, a normal, and a medium-long lens. Having acquired these three objectives, the next step in focal length could be up or down.

After the 105mm, the next most useful focal lengths are 200mm and 300mm—either, not both, since these lenses are not that much different in effect. Generally speaking, 300mm is just about the longest lens you can hand hold in the normal manner. For shooting long-range candid portraits ("the face in the crowd"), 200mm and 300mm are ideal. Lenses of focal lengths longer than 300mm usually are very expensive and may not be used enough by the average photographer to warrant their purchase. There are, however, long telephoto units with which you can have a lot of fun at relatively little cost—prismatic monoculars and telescopes adapted to photographic use. In recent years, there has been a growing interest in telephotography using such instruments in connection with a 35mm SLR camera. The Bushnell TeleVar monocular and Spacemaster telescope give the effects of telephoto lenses in the 350–650mm and 750–3000mm ranges respectively, and the results compare quite favorably with photographs made with conventional telephoto lenses of the same focal lengths, costing up to ten times as much.

The extreme wide-angle 21mm will find little practical application in candid photography, but the 25mm and 28mm focal lengths, covering respectively 4× and 3.2× the 50mm field of view, might come in handy for work in close quarters, as well as in "shooting from the hip," where their extra wide angle of view and great depth of field serve to increase the margin for error in camera pointing. If your normal lens is a 35mm, your wide angle should be a 25mm.

In addition to conventional lenses, the 35mm SLR user also has available to him varifocal or zoom lenses, not made for any other type of still camera. Such objectives offer continuously variable focal length within

HONEYWELL PENTAX H-3, PROFESSIONAL BLACK MODEL, WITH TAKUMAR 200MM *f*/3.5 LENS, an ideal combination for candid shooting at medium long range.

BUSHNELL SPACEMASTER TELEPHOTO UNIT

This is the best scope outfit for telephotography. It consists of the fine Spacemaster 60mm prismatic telescope, 15X eyepiece, and reflex adapter which couples with the body of most 35mm focal-plane-shutter SLR's (camera lens is not used). Equivalent focal-length range with 15X ocular is 750mm to 1500mm; accessory 20X and 25X eyepieces extend range to 3000mm.

BUSHNELL TELEVAR

Companion unit to the Spacemaster is Bushnell's remarkable TeleVar. This compact monocular, only 7″ long and weighing about one lb., is coupled with almost any SLR body by means of an adapter similar to that of the Spacemaster. Equivalent focal-length range is 350mm to 650mm. The TeleVar, although a quality product, costs so little ($59.50) that no SLR user should be without one.

57

NIKKOREX F
WITH AUTO-
NIKKOR ZOOM
43–86MM *f*/3.5

their zoom range. To appreciate the advantages of the zoom lens, you really have to use one for awhile. It offers great possibilities for creative use of the camera—you learn to see pictures in a different way. Frame-filling composition is achieved, not by changing your position back and forth (often disturbing to subjects and deadly to the candid approach), but simply by zooming the lens, varying focal length, until you see the desired cropping of the picture on the ground-glass screen.

By and large, if viewed critically, the quality of photographs produced with zoom lenses is not quite on a par with that which may be achieved with the better fixed focal-length lenses; however, zoom-lens results are certainly acceptable by any normal standards.

The first zoom lens for a 35mm still camera, the Voigtlander-Zoomar introduced in 1959, has a range from 36–82mm. More recent developments in the field of variable focal-length lenses offer zoom ranges of 43–86mm, 80–160mm, 85–250mm, 90–140mm, 95–205mm, and 200–600mm. Which is best for you will depend upon whether you shoot your candids mostly at short, medium, or long range.

Taking into consideration maximum focal length and aperture, the majority of varifocal lenses are fairly large and heavy when compared with fixed focal-length objectives; therefore, in the past, I have hesitated to recommend any zoom lens for general use in candid photography. Now, however, owners of Nikon F and Nikkorex F cameras have available to them a really compact zoom lens covering the range from 43mm* to 86mm, which includes the most-used focal lengths. The Auto-Nikkor Zoom 43–86mm *f*/3.5 lens measures approximately 2¾″ in length and 2½″ in diameter; it weighs about 15 oz. Priced at less than $150, this

---

* This focal length is exactly equal to the diagonal of the 35mm negative, the standard by which the proper normal focal length for a given format is determined.

high-quality zoom lens effectively takes the place of three single lenses that would cost nearly three times as much.

The enticing array of lenses available for 35mm cameras often proves irresistibly tempting and the photographer soon finds himself with a new hobby, lens collecting. He eventually learns that, of his vast optical battery, only a few lenses are used with any degree of regularity. Select additional objectives carefully, with a view to your real needs.

ASTRONAR ZOOM 95–205MM f/6.3

Small size, light weight, and modest price make the Astronar Zoom unique among long varifocal lenses. Its range includes the focal lengths most useful in medium-long-range candid work. Optical quality is excellent. If you are thinking of buying a lens in the focal length range of 95mm to 205mm, give serious consideration to the Astronar Zoom.

A Few Words About Lens Speed

Of recent years, lenses in the f/1 aperture range (e.g., f/0.95, f/1.1, f/1.2) have become available for 35mm cameras. My reaction is, "Who needs them?" Wide open, these lenses exhibit a noticeable lack of definition; center sharpness may be acceptable, but edge fall-off is considerable. Approximate depth of field of a 50mm f/1.1 lens focused at 6' is 3¼"; at this range, 6" (depth of field at f/2) is barely adequate for most purposes. Superspeed lenses of the f/1 class are large, heavy, costly, and of limited usefulness.

If you plan to specialize in available-light photography, you should have a normal lens in the f/1.4 to f/2 range—standard equipment on most 35mm cameras of professional caliber. With a single-lens reflex, it is more important to have a lens of f/2 to f/1.4 aperture than with a rangefinder camera: the brighter image it produces on the SLR's focusing screen is a big help in dim light, especially when a split-image rangefinder is used.

For general use, an f/2.8 or f/3.5 lens is amply fast. After all, the vast majority of exposures are made at median apertures such as f/5.6 and f/8. Don't pay the extra money for a fast lens unless you are sure that you really need it.

59

Peter Basch

Peter Basch

The Twin-Lens Reflex

Next to the 35mm, the 2¼x2¼ twin-lens reflex is the most popular candid camera. Long the workhorse of many top pros, particularly in magazine photography, the 2¼ TLR is now generally conceded to be the predominant press camera—probably because it represents the happy medium between 35mm and 4x5. Wide use by news photographers, here and abroad, certainly attests to the reliability of the twin-lens reflex.

In most respects, the 2¼ TLR is just as well adapted to candid work as are the 35mm rangefinder and single-lens reflex cameras. The average 2¼-square, twin-lens reflex is not significantly larger or heavier than 35mm's of the focal-plane shutter type, especially the single-lens reflexes. It can be handled just as easily, quickly, and inconspicuously.

Probably the major advantages of the 2¼x2¼ twin-lens reflex over 35mm cameras are those of larger format. It is a photographic truism that, all else being equal, the bigger the negative, the less enlargement required, the better the image quality in the final print. The TLR's 2¼-square negatives give usable contact prints and permit greater enlargement, without serious graininess, even when negative color or superspeed black-and-white film has been used. Because of the small 1x1½" negative, good results with 35mm require more care in exposure as well as in the darkroom. In some markets, 2¼x2¼ color transparencies are more saleable than 35mm.

Although the 2¼ TLR's film capacity is not as great as that of the 35mm camera—12 exposures compared with 36—the use of 120 roll film eliminates the need for rewinding the film and, thus, unloading and reloading operations can be carried out in less time than is required with a 35mm.

With the square format it is not necessary to change camera position for horizontal and vertical pictures. The larger ground-glass field makes waist-level focusing feasible. Many candid photographers, who favor the twin-lens reflex, contend that its use at waist level is less likely to attract unwanted attention than is the act of raising a camera to eye level. Waist-level viewing, however, has its disadvantages. Until you become oriented to it, the laterally reversed ground-glass image is quite disconcerting, especially when you try to follow action. Under certain conditions, the ground-glass image is washed out by incident light reaching the screen. With most experienced twin-lens reflex users, the standard procedure is to flip up the magnifier in the hood and hold the camera close to the eye. While this eliminates the overhead-light problem, the previously mentioned advantages of waist-level operation are lost. For eye-level use, the focusing hood of the typical TLR converts to a sports type frame finder, often employed in following action. The standard waist-level focusing hoods of Mamiya and Rollei cameras are interchangeable with eye-level finders: a mirror unit for the former and a pentaprism for the latter; with both types, the ground-glass image is unreversed.

The typical twin-lens reflex has a between-the-lens, leaf type shutter. From a practical standpoint, a good shutter of this kind will perform as

Don Brinn, *AP*. NATALIE WOOD AND GYPSY ROSE LEE ON THE
SET OF THE MOTION PICTURE, "GYPSY."

Wide World Photo

MAMIYA C3
(*left*)

ROLLEIFLEX 2.8F
(*right*)

well as any focal-plane shutter. The former, however, has one major advantage: it affords synchronization at all shutter speeds of all types of flash. While many candid photographers seldom use flash, those who do will regard this feature as a strong point of the 2¼ TLR.

Normal lenses of 2¼-square twin-lens reflexes usually are of 75mm or 80mm focal length; these are best for general use in candid photography. The speeds of TLR lenses may seem slow when compared with the large-aperture objectives available for 35mm cameras, but few occasions will arise where you will have need for a lens faster than the usual $f/3.5$ or $f/2.8$ of these cameras. When it is necessary to work under difficult existing-light conditions, ultra-high-speed films, such as Kodak Royal-X Pan (ASA 1250), can be used; with 2¼x2¼ format, grain is not nearly the problem it is with 35mm. Since $f/2.8$ is almost one stop faster than $f/3.5$, the larger-aperture lens may be well worth having if you plan to do much available-light work.

For years, one of the more frequently voiced objections to twin-lens reflex cameras has been the lack of lens interchangeability and of lenses of other-than-normal focal length. Actually, the experienced TLR user gets along quite nicely with just the standard 75mm or 80mm lens. Using the full negative, he can obtain a wide-angle effect; for a medium-telephoto shot, he can crop to a small portion of the frame. Nevertheless, wide-angle and long-focus lenses often do come in very handy and, in response to the considerable demand, both Mamiya and Rollei now provide them.

The Mamiya Professional C2 and C3 cameras offer lens interchangeability, a feature unique among 2¼x2¼ twin-lens reflexes. Each lens set consists of matched viewing and taking lenses of the same aperture, the latter is mounted in a between-lens shutter; focal lengths include: 65mm, 80mm, 105mm, 135mm, and 180mm. The Mamiya reflexes have bellows with rack and pinion focusing, and are somewhat larger and heavier than

Peter Gowland

conventional 2¼ TLR's such as the Rolleiflex. Film transport is semi-automatic and shutter cocking is a separate operation in the Mamiya cameras. No other TLR offers the great versatility afforded by interchangeable lenses in five focal lengths. With an 80mm *f*/2.8 lens, the Mamiya C3 is priced at less than $250; lens' sets in other focal lengths range from about $100 to $150.

Rollei-Werke has not provided interchangeable lenses, but instead offers separate cameras: the standard Rolleiflex with 75mm or 80mm lens, the wide-angle Rolleiflex with 55mm, and the Tele-Rolleiflex with 135mm. Accessory lens units, Mutar 1.5× and Mutar 0.7×, respectively convert normal 75mm or 80mm Rollei objectives into the equivalents of 112.5mm or 120mm telephoto and 52.5mm or 56mm wide-angle lenses. Introduced some 35 years ago, the Rolleiflex still dominates the professional twin-lens reflex field, although the Japanese have made serious inroads. Well-designed and beautifully made, the Rolleis are compact, moderate in weight, and among the best-handling, fastest-operating still cameras made. There are, at present, eight Rollei models, ranging in price from under $100 to $375. Probably the most popular with advanced candid cameramen is the Rolleiflex 3.5E3 (without built-in meter), priced at less than $250.

The choice between a Mamiya Professional and one of the Rolleiflex models will depend largely upon the importance to you of lens interchangeability. To those shopping for a 2¼ TLR in the under-$100 bracket, I recommend consideration of Minolta, Ricoh, and Yashica cameras, good optically as well as mechanically, and moderately priced.

A half-dozen or so years ago, famed glamour photographer Peter Gowland designed a large-format, twin-lens reflex camera, which was

GOWLANDFLEX

Peter Gowland

built originally for his own use. After five years of regular use, testing, and improvement, the perfected Gowlandflex went into production and is now on the market. Offered in 4x5 and 5x7 models, the Gowlandflex combines the advantages of the twin-lens reflex with those of large format. Its forte, of course, is pictures of people. Because the photographer can keep his subject in constant view, can compose and focus right up to the moment of exposure, it is possible to achieve with the Gowlandflex the desirable "candid" quality so difficult to obtain with a view camera, even when working with experienced models. The Gowlandflex is the ideal large-format candid camera for those who regularly work with a 2¼x2¼ TLR.

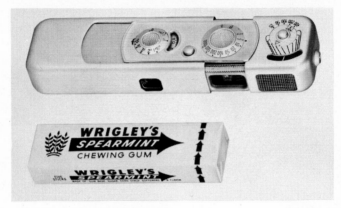

MINOX B

The Subminiature Camera

How many "never-again" picture opportunities have you missed because you didn't have a camera with you? The answer to this question usually provides the best argument for owning a subminiature camera, which can be carried conveniently at all times.

A subminiature is a camera designed for film narrower than 35mm. Nearly all current subminiatures use 16mm cine film and the usual negative size is 10x14mm. The notable exception is the Minox which produces 8x11mm negatives on 9.5mm film. Although some efforts are being made toward standardization of film cassettes, at present each camera has its own system, not compatible with any other. With the exception of those for the Minox, the cassettes are readily reloaded with bulk film. Large camera stores ordinarily stock factory-loaded cassettes for the Minox and other popular subminiatures.

Most people, on becoming interested in subminiature photography, inquire as to picture quality and degree of enlargement possible. Precision subminiatures are capable of excellent results. While wallet-size prints

68

may be the practical limit of enlargement of negatives on super-fast film exposed under poor available-light conditions, most good subminiature negatives can be enlarged to 4x5 or 5x7; those on slower, thin-emulsion films often may be blown up to 8x10. Bear in mind that a 10x14mm (16mm) negative requires a linear enlargement of 10× to produce a 4x5 print, the equivalent of making an 11x14 from a 24x36mm (35mm) negative. Obviously, some allowance should be made for the limitations of very small format when judging quality. Since margins for error narrow with decrease in negative size, a little more care is required with the subminiature in every operation from loading the camera to making the print.

The Minox is the best known and most widely used subminiature camera—the number of its users now runs well into six figures. Its very small size and complete dependability make this camera especially well suited to candid use. The current Minox B, with built-in exposure meter, measures only 3⅞x1⅛x⅝″ and weighs a mere 3¼ oz. It has a 15mm *f*/3.5 lens of fixed aperture (designed for best performance at *f*/3.5, this objective needs no diaphragm). Shutter speeds range from 1/2 to 1/1000 sec. Film loads are 36- or 50-exposure. This is the world's smallest precision camera and truly a masterpiece of miniaturization. The Minox B sells for under $150.

By far the best of the 16mm's is the unique GaMi, a connoisseur's subminiature which includes virtually every camera feature imaginable and offers the most completely accessorized system of its kind; price is about $300. There are a number of good, moderately-priced, 16mm subminiatures, among them the Mamiya, Mec, Mikroma, and Minolta; these range in price from less than $25 to about $100.

GAMI 16

For the candid photographer who wants a readily pocketable camera but finds the limitations of 16mm format too restrictive for his purposes, there are the compact half-frame cameras—subminiature 35mm's. Most such cameras use standard 35mm film cartridges for twice the usual number of exposures, negative size being 18x24mm instead of 24x36mm. The typical half-frame camera measures about 1" smaller all around than the conventional 35mm; a 28 to 32mm normal lens, partially recessed in the camera body, contributes to its slimness.

Pioneer in the half-frame field is Japan's Olympus Optical Co., whose Pen series—including a very interesting single-lens reflex—is the best known line of 18x24mm cameras. Other attractive half-frame models include the handsomely styled Canon Demi and the completely automated Ricoh Auto Half. Smallest 35mm camera on the market today is the Tessina, a 2½x2x1", 5-ounce, twin-lens reflex from Switzerland. This camera, which can easily hide inside a cigarette package, uses standard 35mm film in a special cassette; negative size is 14x21mm, somewhat smaller than half-frame format but twice as large as the typical 16mm still camera negative.

Certainly the most unobtrusive of cameras by virtue of very small size, the subminiatures are ideal for undercover candid photography, as well as being cameras you can *wear* at all times.

To those readers who are interested in subminiature photography, I suggest my book, *Subminiature Technique* (The Modern Camera Guide Series, Chilton Books), a complete manual on the subject.

TESSINA 35MM "SUBMINIATURE"

Peter Gowland

The Polaroid Land Camera

Whenever I am asked to recommend a camera for general family use, I always suggest a Polaroid Land camera. These cameras are very easy to use and anyone, even a child, can take good pictures with one of the current electric-eye models. It's really just as simple as it looks in Polaroid's TV commercials. Results are, by and large, on a par with those obtainable with the conventional photographic process and the cost is about the same. The great attractiveness of the Polaroid Land process is, of course, the fact that it makes possible *instant pictures*. Seeing the print 10 seconds after the picture is taken makes photography twice as much fun. Although effective automatic exposure control and virtually foolproof operation minimize the chances of such occurrences, *if, at first, you don't succeed*, you'll know it right away and you can *try again*—something that isn't possible with any other system of photography.

Polaroid Land cameras are not, however, just for the "box-camera set." I believe that I qualify as a serious photographer and I am a constant user of a Polaroid Land camera. It has proved a real lifesaver on numerous occasions when a print was needed right away. Aside from its many practical applications, the Polaroid Land camera has provided me with a great deal of pleasure. It's something different from the conventional cameras that are my tools, and the novelty of it hasn't palled. I strongly urge every serious photographer to add a Polaroid Land camera to his equipment (after using it for awhile, you'll wonder how you ever got along without it).

For making friends and influencing otherwise camera-shy people to let you take pictures, the Polaroid Land camera is a "must" in the traveler's kit. Often, a personable assistant, thus equipped, can hold the subject's attention with the magic of instant pictures while you shoot away, unnoticed, with your conventional camera.

Although the Polaroid Land cameras, with the exception of the compact Model J33, aren't small in size, they can be used candidly if the photographer has learned to work unobtrusively. Best and most versatile of the current Polaroid Land electric-eye cameras is Model 900. Its features include automatic exposure control via a super-sensitive, cadmium-sulphide cell (with option of manual control when desired), coupled rangefinder and parallax-corrected viewfinder combined in one window, built-in synchronization for flashbulbs, strobe, and Wink Light. Price is less than $160. For those who would like an even simpler and/or lower-priced Polaroid camera, there are the J66, like Model 900, a 3¼x4¼, and the smaller J33, which makes 2½x3¼ prints. These models are fixed focus, have the very easy to operate "1–2–3–4" button control system, and exposure is set automatically by selenium-cell electric eye. Model J33 is priced at under $75 and the J66 costs about $25 more.

Polaroid 3000 Speed Land Picture Roll is ideal for available-light work. Its ASA equivalent exposure index of 3200 makes possible indoor picture taking by ordinary room light. Development time is 10 seconds. The revolutionary Polaroid Land color film, Polacolor, produces a finished color

Kralik Andory. CZARDAS. Hungary, c. 1939. Rolleicord Photo.

Courtesy Rollei-Werke

POLAROID J66

print in 50 seconds. ASA equivalent exposure index is 75. Indoor pictures with Polacolor film can be made with blue flashbulbs, or a blue shield over white flashbulbs, or with electronic flash. Type 48 Polacolor film for 3¼x4¼ pictures can be used in all existing Land cameras using 40-series film. Type 38 Polacolor film for 2½x3¼ pictures can be used in the Model J33 cameras.

All Polaroid Land equipment and materials are well designed for easy use and are accompanied by complete, readily understood instructions. If these simple directions are read carefully and followed to the letter, the results are excellent.

POLAROID 900

Fritz Peyer. LA GRANDE DAME DE LA DANSE.

Exposure Meters

Probably more photographs are ruined by exposure errors than by all other causes of failure combined. Because of the wide latitude of some modern films, you can get by, occasionally, without using an exposure meter, substituting experience and/or luck; however, for consistently good results under all conditions, there is no substitute for a reliable exposure meter. It must, of course, be handled properly and the readings interpreted intelligently. Effective use of an exposure meter is not difficult to learn from the excellent instruction booklets furnished with all of the better instruments. While a reasonably good photoelectric exposure meter can be bought for less than $10, the serious photographer, who uses a top-quality camera, certainly should equip himself with a top-quality exposure meter. Next to the camera, the exposure meter is the most important piece of photographic equipment.

The two basic types of exposure meter are the photoelectric (selenium cell) and the photoconductive (cadmium-sulphide cell). In the more common photoelectric exposure meters, light striking the selenium cell generates electric current which, in turn, deflects the galvanometer needle. The newer, photoconductive type operates on a different principle: the electric eye is a cadmium-sulphide (CdS) cell that changes its conductivity in the presence of light. A tiny mercury battery is connected to a galvanometer with a CdS cell placed in the circuit where it offers resistance to the flow of electricity in relation to the intensity of the light falling on the cell—the more light, the greater the amount of electric current allowed to pass through to the galvanometer; the indicator needle is, of course, deflected accordingly. With either type of meter, the exposure index of the film having been set, the position of the needle indicates directly, or after transfer of the reading to computer on the meter, the combinations of lens aperture and shutter speed which will give correct exposure.

Greater sensitivity at low light levels is the CdS meter advantage of most importance to the candid photographer, who frequently works under

LUNASIX

SPECTRA COMBI-500

76

Robert Fréson

Courtesy Popular Photography Magazine

poor existing-light conditions. With today's very fast lenses and high-speed films, if there is enough light for you to see the subject, you usually can photograph him—*provided that the correct exposure can be determined.* Conventional photoelectric exposure meters, while adequate for general use, are not sufficiently sensitive (the selenium cell cannot generate enough current to deflect the meter needle to a significant degree) to provide usably accurate readings at the lowest light levels under which photography is now possible. The battery-powered, cadmium-sulphide-cell meters, up to several hundred times more sensitive than the average selenium-cell meter, afford the extreme low-light sensitivity and accuracy required for successful available-light photography under all conditions.

Exposure meters measure either reflected light, the light reflected from the subject, or incident light, the light which falls on that part of the subject which is facing the camera. Both methods of light measurement give satisfactory results, if properly employed. By means of accessory converters, most reflected-light meters may be used to read incident light and incident-light meters to read reflected light; however, each type of meter does best with the method of light measurement for which it was primarily designed. I have found only one meter that measures both incident and reflected light with equal facility and accuracy—the Gossen Lunasix, a super-sensitive CdS meter.

It is the common practice, especially when using a camera with a built-in exposure meter, to take all reflected-light readings from the photographing position. Because of the wide acceptance angle of the average reflected-light meter, which integrates much of the brightness or darkness outside the important picture areas, such over-all readings frequently result in serious exposure errors. In many situations, it is advisable, if not imperative, that readings be taken with the meter held close to the subject. Where this is not feasible, as is usually the case in candid work, the photographer must take substitute close-up readings, for example, from the palm of his hand.

With an incident-light meter, the white, hemispherical light collector is pointed toward the camera from the subject position. This instrument measures the total illumination falling on the subject from all angles, side and front; it evaluates this illumination and indicates an exposure which will most readily duplicate the relative brightness of the various parts of the subject as seen by the human eye. In effect, the light collector serves as stand-in for the person to be photographed. Where illumination at the camera position is identical to the lighting of the subject, the reading may be taken near the camera, provided that the light collector is held at the same angle with respect to the illumination as it would be if at subject position, pointed at the camera. If the camera and subject positions are not receiving equal illumination, reading must be taken at the subject position. In candid photography, it usually is advisable to make advance light measurements in the area where you expect to take pictures. I have found that this can be accomplished most efficiently and inconspicuously with an incident-light meter. Although it may take a bit longer to learn

Fee Schlapper. THE ANTIQUE BROOCH.

the proper use of this instrument, once mastered, it is the quickest and easiest meter to use, as well as the most reliable. Best of the incident-light exposure meters is the Spectra Combi-500, a professional instrument widely used in the motion picture industry and equally well adapted to still photography. This meter incorporates both a selenium cell for normal conditions and a battery-powered, ultra-sensitive, photoconductive cell for low-light situations. Its sensitivity, 500 times that of the average selenium-cell meter, is limited only by total darkness.

There are times when you cannot get near enough to the subject position to take close-up readings with a conventional reflected-light meter or to use an incident-light meter effectively and illumination conditions are such that usable substitute readings are not possible. This is frequently the case in telephoto work. When the subject is in surroundings of strongly contrasting brightness (for example, a spot-lighted performer on the stage of an otherwise dark theatre), the over-all reading given by a conventional reflected-light meter, held at a distant camera position, will indicate an incorrect exposure. Even the 30° measuring area of the Gossen Lunasix may prove too large under such conditions and this acceptance angle is less than half that of the usual reflected-light meter. For these situations, the exposure meter must have a very narrow light acceptance angle and be provided with a means of accurate aiming at the subject. I have found the most practical solution of this problem to be the Honeywell Pentax 3°/21°, a CdS spot meter for reflected-light readings. This instrument looks like a miniature waist-level, single-lens reflex camera. The subject is viewed through a 100mm lens via a reflex mirror and chimney type magnifying hood. Field of view of the circular ground-glass screen is 21°; a small circle in its center defines the 3° area covered by the meter. Reading is taken from a scale below the center spot on the ground glass and transferred to a calculator ring on the lens mount, where lens-aperture and shutter-speed combinations are indicated. One of the easier meters to use, the Honeywell 3°/21° also is very accurate and sufficiently sensitive for all but the more extreme low-light situations. It really is a must for any photographer who often shoots candids at long range.

Summing up my exposure meter recommendations, I feel that the candid photographer is well advised to use a CdS meter because of its greatly superior low-light sensitivity. For general use, involving both reflected- and incident-light readings, I consider the Gossen Lunasix to be by far the best choice. When meter readings can be taken at subject position or another spot receiving similar illumination, which is the case most of the time, my preference is for an incident-light meter, the Spectra Combi-500. For long-range work, the Honeywell 3°/21° is pretty much in a class by itself.

What about built-in exposure meters? Generally speaking, I am of the opinion that the serious candid photographer, especially the available-light worker, needs the greater sensitivity and versatility of use afforded by the better separate meters, particularly those of the CdS type. With a

Fee Schlapper. AT A TAXI WINDOW IN COLOMBO.

HONEYWELL 3/21

built-in meter, there is a considerable temptation to take all readings from the camera position. In a contrasty lighting situation, the average, over-all reading thus obtained will result in incorrect exposure. Even experienced photographers tend to neglect proper exposure determination practices when using on-camera meters.

Films for Candid Photography

To avoid confusion, the candid photographer is well advised to standardize on a few films. It is suggested that personal exposure indexes be established for the preferred films. To determine the correct exposure index for a particular film with your camera and meter, make a series of test shots (with subject and lighting unchanged) at indexes bracketing the official ASA number. Note that the exposure index is doubled when you use the next faster shutter speed at the same lens aperture or the next smaller aperture at the same speed. It is advisable to vary the lens aperture and retain the same shutter speed throughout the series of test shots. Exposures at the basic reading obtained by using the official exposure index, two stops over, and three or four stops under, should be sufficient. Incidentally, this same series of tests will serve to illustrate the effective latitude of the film.

Medium-speed, black-and-white films, offering good exposure latitude (up to 3 stops underexposure is tolerated), are best suited to general use with a 35mm camera. Higher speed films should be reserved for those occasions when limited light and/or fast action demand their use. I have standardized on Kodak Plus-X Pan (ASA 160*), which I use in most of my 35mm black-and-white work, switching to Kodak Tri-X Pan (ASA 400*) when light conditions require a faster film. The slower lens and larger format of the 2¼x2¼ twin-lens reflex suggest the advisability of adopting films such as Tri-X Pan for general use and Kodak Royal-X Pan (ASA 1250*) for available-light work with this type of camera.

* Exposure indexes indicated are standard; these films can be safely re-rated at 2× these indexes, but the tests previously outlined should be made.

Eugeen Warmenbol

Courtesy Popular Photography Magazine

Kodachrome II and Kodachrome X are the outstanding color films and, because of the fine results obtainable, should be used whenever possible. Exposure indexes of 25 and 64, however, limit the use of Kodachrome films in poor light. Where available-light work requires a faster color film, I recommend Kodak High-Speed Ektachrome, Daylight (EI 160) or Type B (EI 125), depending upon the nature of the illumination. Kodachrome is not available in 120 size, but High-Speed Ektachrome is; you will find the latter a good choice for general use with 2¼x2¼ cameras.

ULTRABLITZ MONOJET UM   HONEYWELL STROBONAR II

Flash Units

As a general rule, candid photographers prefer to work by available light. Such photos have an appealing quality of naturalness often lacking in flash pictures. Furthermore, once the flash is fired, it is difficult for the photographer to remain "candid." There are times, however, when the existing light is too dim to permit picture taking with the lens and/or film in use—this is more often true with a twin-lens reflex than with a 35mm because of the slower lenses of the former. I think that every photographer should equip himself with a flash unit, if only to be prepared for such emergencies.

When electronic-flash equipment became reasonably compact, I discontinued the use of flashbulbs. Not having to carry pocketfuls of bulbs and not having to change bulbs between shots are conveniences of electronic flash that I really appreciate. The speed of an electronic flash exposure—1/1000 sec. with most of the compact units—contributes to the picture quality by minimizing the effects of camera and subject movement. The short duration of the flash makes it easier on the subject's eyes than are ordinary flashbulbs. If you do a fair amount of flash photography,

Joseph Alpern, *Sid Avery Associates.* THEY JUST DON'T MAKE STAGECOACHES LIKE THEY USED TO.

Mattel Toymakers of Hawthorne, California, used this clever "candid" in a recent advertisement featuring the authentically styled toy carbine and sixshooter they make for the small-fry cowboy trade.

you will find that it is more economical to own a strobe unit than it is to buy flashbulbs at a dime or so apiece.

Today, there are available small, lightweight, one-piece, electronic-flash units, eliminating the need for a separate power.pack; these easily fit in a coat pocket and take up very little room in the gadget bag. Units of this type include: Braun F21, Heliotron MM, Metz 109 and 110, Ultrablitz Monojet UM. Intended for accessory-shoe mounting, these are more suitable for use with 35mm cameras than with twin-lens reflexes. The Honeywell Strobonars, which are attached by means of bracket and quick-release clamp, are ideally suited to twin-lens reflex cameras; since the flash head has a convenient handle, this unit is easier to use for off-camera and bounce-flash techniques.

For flattering, virtually shadow-free lighting of informal portraits, the unique Hershey Sun Ring provides an excellent light source. This "around-the-lens" unit, a larger version of the electronic-flash ring lights often employed in close-up photography, is fitted to single-lens reflex, press, view, and Polaroid cameras by means of a standard adapter ring. It may be used with almost any power pack of up to 200 watt-seconds output. The Sun Ring is quite compact and weighs only 5 ounces.

HERSHEY
SUN RING

Jean-Philippe Charbonnier

Réalités

The Candid Tape Recorder

Quite often, during the course of a shooting session, remarks are made by the subject that might be used effectively in picture captions or possibly incorporated in an article accompanying the photos. It usually isn't feasible for the photographer to make notes in the midst of picture-taking (and this might be disturbing to the subject). To rely on memory is risky; at least I find it so. On such occasions, a small, portable tape recorder is useful. It can turn an ordinary, informal portrait session into an interesting photo-interview.

The photographer will soon find many other applications for his tape recorder as a camera adjunct. For example: think how much on-the-spot recordings would enliven your color-slide showings of vacation, travel, sports, and party pictures, etc. There are available a number of tape recorders small enough to be concealed, if you so desire; the ethics of candid recording I leave up to the reader.

WEBCOR MICROCORDER II

Ideal for candid recording, the Microcorder is compact enough to fit in gadget bag or brief case. This all-transistor tape recorder measures 8x8x2⁵⁄₁₆ in. and weighs just a shade over 4 lb. Performance is outstanding for a recorder of this type.

Hilde Moray. NEWSPAPER VENDOR, PIGALLE.

Irmtraud Hermann

Werner Schmoelcke   Zeiss Ikon Photo.

Courtesy Zeiss Ikon AG.

Pal-Nils Nilsson. VIA APPIA.

Tiofoto

Pal-Nils Nilsson. CONEY ISLAND.

Tiofoto

Rudi Herzog. BEAUTY QUEENS.

4. EPILOGUE

As was said in the beginning, it is the intent of this book to provide an introduction to the art of the candid camera, its basic techniques and matériel. No other branch of photography demands a more complete mastery of the camera. Equipment must be selected with careful consideration and the techniques of its operation practiced until they become almost automatic. Only then can the photographer devote his full attention to the capture of "the decisive moment." A good candid photograph is much more than a mere record; it is a profound expression of the artist's way of seeing and thinking. This is too personal an art to be taught effectively—you must learn it by yourself. If this book succeeds occasionally in pointing some neophyte candid photographer in the right direction, it will have fulfilled its purpose.

Hilmar Pabel. CHINESISCHE VOLKSWEISHEIT.